The festival of life; pictures of man, woman & child

Kanu Desai

FESTIVAL OF LIFE

PICTURES OF MAN WOMAN & CHILD

By Kanu Desai

JEEVAN MANGAL

THE FESTIVAL OF LIFE

PICTURES OF MAN WOMAN & CHILD

BY

KANU DESAI

D. B. TARAPOREVALA SONS & Co. HORNBY ROAD · BOMBAY-1

Printed By B P Rawat at Kumar printery, 1454 Raipur, Ahmedabad and
Published by Kanu Desai at Kumar Karyalaya Ltd , 1454 Raipur, Ahmedabad

To

Jayantilal Thakore
Pranlal Thakore
Jagatprasad Thakore

CONTENTS

FESTIVAL OF LIFE

KANU Desai conceives lovely visions of life and sets them on paper in his inimitable way. He weaves the daily world of experience in silent poetic numbers. His mind which created before, the exquisite 'Pictures of Love, Life and Marriage', as a preliminary to conjugal life is now enraptured by its actual experience and expresses itself in a fresh creation, 'The Festival of Life.' His clear-seeing artistic eye is able to discern that the human child is not merely an outcome of sex attraction but is an ambrosial essence issuing from the inmost springs of the soul. The observers of the accompanying pictures, it is expected, will experience the sweet fragrance spreading forth from the Divine Garden of the Great Dispenser and not the dream of secret and occasional human dalliance.

In the very first picture entitled 'Gift' the artist sets forth a young wife returning from paternal home after the first child-birth. She presents 'the immortal art of the soul' to her eager young husband, who extends his arms of welcome to the new life, with eyes feasting on the beloved's face in ecstatic joy. Look carefully at the face of the young lady. What is occupying her thoughts at the moment? She may be speaking to herself "Here is our 'dear delight' for whom our elders propitiated great many gods and goddesses. Here is the result of our soul's union." Even to a casual onlooker of lines in these pictures, it is needless to dilate upon details regarding the wonderful unity of facts, emotion and technique.

The next picture is 'the cradle' which reveals the real poetry of life flowing from the same fountain of emotional unity. Here is a mother plunged in delcious dreams holding the string of the cradle while her darling is asleep. The juxtaposition of characters and the lines depicting the surrounding world are entirely appropriate. A mere glimpse of the baby's fore-head from the cradle presents picture of perfect loveliness. Herein lies the characteristic style of Kanu.

'Grandmother' is the title of the third picture. This venerable old lady showers her choicests blessings upon her dearest who is spreading sunshine in the life of the newly wedded pair. She seems to set aside the burden of life she has so long endured and finds freshness and peace in the cheerful company of the child. She forgets disparity of age and is lost in raptures in his artless lispings and innocent play.

In the fourth picture 'Initiation' the artist exhibits the house-steps which symbolise the child's embarking upon life's journey. A present-day cultured Gujarati mother is represented in an environment of domestic bliss to the ample credit of the artist.

The fifth picture which is styled 'Divine Grace' shows that notwithstanding the numerous researches of science, every affectionate soul is bound to beseech best luck to the dearest ones by invoking the Invisible Power. If mass prayers are celebrated for the welfare of the royal princes, it is not at all surprising when a mother pacifies her mind before the placid image of the Supreme Deity in the interest of her own darling. This picture stands forth as a unique sample of serene power and quiet conception. The artist had suddenly seized an altogether new point of view. It is a splendid example of originality and bold delineation. Though the eye clearly sees the difference between the stone image and the animating characters yet it is the force of the former which fills the whole atmosphere.

The sixth picture is a successful piece of Kanu Desai's suggestive art. The blissful mother delighted with the sportive trick of her darling is submerged in the flood of joy bursting forth from his laughter. How artistically the Gujarati lady is delineated with a few strokes of simple lines! A glance from her head to hand which is poised on the ground makes us forget the lines but acquaints us full with her gentle and graceful person And her attire does not consist of mere cuts of lines Her sparse-woven Sâri with its soft folds, adorning the life of Gujarat is a beautiful illustration of the artist's observation This is the most novel composition in the whole series. There are plenty of pictures which surprise the eye with dazzling brilliance, but Kanu's pictures being conceived with some rare skill are full of charm and delight

The seventh picture consists of 'A fairy Tale'. There is an hour of the Indian night, a little after sunset, when the heat and disquiet of the day have ended, wherein a deep and mystic atmosphere thickens which inspires imagination and creates a world of dreams From times immemorial, this mystieal outlook has given birth to innumerable tales and folk-tales of infinite interest and the greatest credit goes to the child as the inspirer. It is the child who spurs the mother's imagination and the latter is obliged to create endless forms of fancy The present picture reveals this pleasant fact and is a living embodiment of poetry impregnated with Indian culture and rare simplicity. With what curiosity and sense of wonder the child is looking at the figure of a beautiful fairy flashing on the mother's face! It is indeed certain that a child derives greater pleasures from fairy tales then those from vast empires

In the musical lines of the eighth pictures entitled 'Festival of Life' is glorified the human child who consecrates the garden of this world Life loses all its flavour if man cannot feel the melody of child's flute. It is the child who helps each and all, whether king or pauper, rich or penniless, to realise the shining vision of life The youthful pair of this picture enjoys the rhythmic dance of that everlasting song of life in tune with the child' The artist has intensified the interest by proper and adequate lines. Let this music pervade the whole world like the rapidly emerging lines of this picture

It is impossible to express the universal purpose in man's imperfect utterance. It can however, be realised in the reciprocal love-creations of living beings It is only here that life becomes a festival.

May this picture-series spread the melodious strains of that music in every home

Ratilal M Trivedi

The Gift
प्रथम पुष्प

The Cradle हालरडं

Grand-mother

दादीमा

Initiation

पा-पा पगली

Divine Grace

বাঘা

Sweet Annoyance मस्ती

Fairy Tale परीकथा

Festival of Life　　　　जीवन मंगल

From the
Pen Pencil and Brush
of
KANU DESAI

SILHOUETTES
Part I Part II
WATER COLOURS
Part I Part II
NRITYA REKHA
RANGA LAHARI
Part I Part II
LAGNOTSAVA
MANGALASHTAKA
FESTIVAL OF LIFE
FOLK-RITUALS
MAHATMA GANDHI
INDIA'S PILGRIMAGE
MIRABAI
RUPREKHA
SHREE LEKHA
SHRINGARIKA
INDIAN LANDSCAPES

In Preparation
PRANAYA MADHURI
UMAR KHAYYAM
GITA-GOVINDA
RAMAYANA
SEASONS

卐

To be had from
Kumar Karyalaya Ltd Ahmedabad
D. B Taraporevala Sons & Co.
Bombay

Rs. 3-0-0

CPSIA information can be obtained at www.ICGtesting.com
Printed in the USA
LVOW01s1513051015

456963LV00015BA/320/P